CAT CHAMPIONS

CARING FOR OUR
FELINE FRIENDS

ROB LAIDLAW

pajamapress

CONTENTS

Wherever people live, you'll find cats. Settling near humans for thousands of years, cats were kept as pets in ancient Rome and honored in ancient Egypt. Today, cats are kept as pets around the world. Cat shows display the most beautiful—and unusual—purebreds. Pet stores sell everything from the smallest cat toy to elaborate scratching posts, water fountains, and even artificial trees to play on. Cat lovers give their pets lots of love and attention and the best food and medical care they can afford.

But not every cat has a loving owner. There is another world of cats out there. Pet cats become lost or abandoned and must fend for themselves. Feral cats who have not been spayed or neutered give birth, producing more homeless cats, sometimes

in large numbers. Neglected cats can become sick or injured. Animal shelters cannot find homes for all the cats they receive; many shelters destroy cats that are not adopted out quickly. Even in countries where cats are not kept as pets, there are many cats struggling to survive on the streets or in the wild. The life of a homeless cat can be brutal and short.

For anyone who cares about cats, there's a lot to be concerned about. But there is also a reason to hope. Thousands of people around the world are doing their part to help cats. You'll find many organizations on the Internet. But individuals young and old can help by donating money, volunteering at shelters, fostering, adopting, or even starting an organization or a campaign to help cats. I call these people Cat Champions, and together they save hundreds of thousands of cats. I want to tell you about a few of the kids around the world who have become Cat Champions. When you read their stories, I think you'll be inspired to find your own way to help cats. You'll also learn about what it takes to rescue, foster, socialize, and adopt cats and kittens

Cats need our kindness, respect, love, and action. I'm confident that, one by one, we can make the world a better place for our feline friends.

– ROB

Cats are very acrobatic

Meet Felis Catus

Today's cats are classified as being in the *Felidae* family and that's why they are sometimes referred to as *felids*. Domesticated cats are known by the scientific name *Felis catus*. And they are easy to identify. They have a sleek, powerful body, a relatively broad head, short muzzle, and sharp, specialized teeth. They have 5 toes on their front paws, including the dewclaw on their leg, 4 toes on their rear paws, and 28-30 teeth; but their weight, size, color, and kind of fur can vary considerably. There's no such thing as an average domesticated cat.

The Cat's Out of the Bag

Is it true that a falling cat always lands on his feet? With their long flexible backbones, cats have a remarkable ability to correct their position in the air so they land feet first. But that does not mean cats cannot be injured in a fall; they can still break bones or even die from an extreme fall.

Quick reflexes allow cats to move quickly

Leaping is a regular part of cat life

The CAT'S MEOW

Which animals jump higher, cats or dogs? If you guessed cats, you are right. An average dog can jump about as high as her body length. But a cat can jump five or six times her body length in one giant leap.

Cats have extraordinary balance

Cats have evolved to crawl, walk, squeeze, run, climb, and jump. They have powerful muscles and fast reflexes, an excellent sense of smell, eyesight that allows them to see well in dim or dark conditions, and sensitive whiskers. They can hear high-pitched sounds, like those made by mice and other rodents. Of course, these are all things that a successful nighttime predator would need to survive; and that's exactly what cats are—predators. That doesn't mean all cats have to hunt, but it does mean they need lots of exercise and space to move about.

WHAT DOES IT MEAN WHEN I…?

Here are some cat sounds and what they mean:

When I purr…I'm happy or afraid.

When I meow…I want you humans to do something for me!

When I trill (a sound between a purr and a meow)…I'm saying hello.

When I hiss…I'm afraid and I'm telling you to stay back.

When I rumble or growl…I'm telling you to get out of my territory.

When I chatter or chirp (a sound between a meow and a bleat)… I'm looking at prey I can't catch, like a bird or insect. And I want it!

Cats are independent and can be solitary or social, usually choosing their own companions. Some cats establish a territory and mark their boundaries with urine, feces, and scratching.

Many people think cats are quiet and keep to themselves, but they have a wide variety of communication methods. My own cat Twister will meow like crazy when he wants something. There are other sounds that cats make as well, including purrs, hisses, growls, and screeches. But that's not all. Cats also communicate with body postures, facial expressions, and their ear and tail positions. It's easy to tell what a cat thinks when she meets a strange dog—she may turn sideways, arch her back, raise the fur on her body and tail to look bigger, flatten her ears against her head, and hiss and growl. The cat is telling the dog to keep back.

Cats who lie on their backs feel comfortable and safe

Cats use body postures, like arching their backs, to send a message

Most cats know how to stalk prey

The CAT'S MEOW

Just how good is a cat's sight? In daylight, cats see almost as well as humans. At night, however, cats have much better vision than we do. Their pupils are elliptical: they are long and thin and can open much faster than human pupils; this allows more light to enter the eye. And cat vision is designed to detect motion, which is great for hunting.

When it's dark, a cat's pupils open wide to let in light

When it's bright, the pupils become narrow slits

Cats are highly intelligent animals. Wild cats and feral domesticated cats have to use their wits and intelligence to survive in very complex environments. If they weren't smart, they wouldn't be able to survive.

Most cats are predators that can hunt even if they've grown up indoors. They usually hunt alone and will spend a lot of time searching for and stalking prey or sitting and waiting for a prey animal to appear, such as when a mouse sticks its head out of the opening of a burrow. Cats are opportunistic predators, which means they'll hunt a lot of different kinds of prey, such as insects, reptiles, birds, rodents, and other animals.

A Fabulous Assortment of Felines

There are at least 40 recognized cat breeds and they come in every size, shape, and color. They may have long hair, short hair, or no hair. Their tails can be long, short, or not there at all. They can have large or small bodies, a normal muzzle, or a flat face. Some cats have long ears, while others have short ears or weird curled ears.

Some cat breeds are extremely old. The Egyptian Mau and the Abyssinian cat are thought to have originated in ancient Egypt thousands of years ago. The Japanese Bobtail cat, the Siamese and Korat cats of Thailand, the Angora of Turkey, and the Norwegian Forest cat are also very old. In North America, the Maine Coon was first identified over 150 years ago. And the modern Canadian Sphynx, a nearly hairless cat, only dates back about 50 years.

Bengal cat

Persian

A modern Canadian Sphynx

Maine Coon

Ragdoll kittens have blue eyes and long hair

Savannah cats are a hybrid cat breed

Cats On Display

With so many cats in the world, it's not surprising that there are also a lot of cat shows. Hundreds of local, regional, national, and international cat shows take place in countries across the globe every year. A cat show is simply an event in which cats are judged, usually to see which individual cat comes closest to meeting its breed standard. But in addition to displaying pedigreed cats, some shows also permit regular companion cats to enter. They're placed into categories, such as the All Breed Category. Other categories can include long hair and short hair breeds, or even cats of different ages. The rules for cat shows can vary, depending on where they take place, so there's really no such thing as a typical cat show.

Show cats wait to be judged

Cool Cats: The Hemingway Cats

Between 1931 and 1939, the American author Ernest Hemingway owned a house in Key West, Florida. Famed for great works of literature like *The Sun Also Rises*, *The Old Man and the Sea*, and *A Farewell to Arms*, Hemingway died in 1961. His home in Florida is now a national historic site, which attracts 250,000 visitors every year. More than 40 polydactyl cats roam the house and property. Many people believe the cats are descended from a six-toed cat named Snowball, a ship captain's gift to Hemingway in the early 1930s. The cats go wherever they please, and the museum staff cares for them. In 2005 the United States Department of Agriculture called in the agency PETA (People for the Ethical Treatment of Animals) to make sure the cats were properly treated; the investigator confirmed the cats were "fat, happy, and relaxed."

The Cat's Out
of the Bag

Cats normally have 18 toes: 5 toes on each front foot and 4 toes on each back foot. Polydactylism (which means "many-fingered") is a genetic mutation, not a special breed. Polydactyl cats usually have more digits on their front feet, but some cats have extra digits on their hind feet too. It's rare to find a polydactyl cat with extra toes on all four feet. In 2002, the *Guinness Book of World Records* recognized Jake, a cat from Canada, for the greatest number of toes: 7 on each paw, for a total of 28!

A polydactyl paw

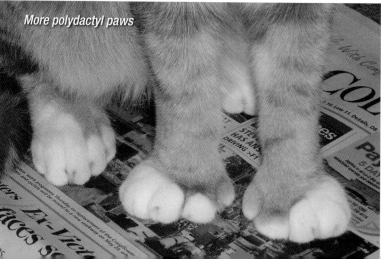

More polydactyl paws

A "Hemingway Cat"

The CAT'S MEOW

Most cats hate water, but they can happily live on boats. And the tradition of keeping a cat on board a ship goes back thousands of years. Cats were carried on trading ships to catch mice and rats, which could carry disease, ruin shipments, and chew through ropes and woodwork.

Cool Cats: Simon the War Cat

In 1948, when Simon was a year old, a sailor smuggled him aboard the British Royal Navy warship *Amethyst*. Simon was popular with the crew, especially for catching rats on the ship's lower decks. He often slept in the captain's hat and he left dead rat "presents" in the sailors' beds. In 1949, the *Amethyst* sailed up China's Yangtze River toward Nanking and was involved in a battle. Simon was seriously injured by an exploding bomb. He crawled along the deck until crewmembers could get him below and treat his shrapnel injuries. After a few weeks, the lower decks were overrun with rats. Once Simon recovered, he resumed his duties. He's credited with saving the crew's food supply and inspiring the seamen. Simon was given many awards, including the prestigious Dickin Medal for gallantry and devotion to duty.

Simon the War Cat

It's an
Alley Cat World

The Cat's Out of the Bag

How many cats are there in the world? Although it's impossible to know for sure, estimates place the number of cats worldwide at around 600 million. In North America alone, there are around 86 million cats that are owned. If you add feral cats, the total number of cats living in North America could be 172 million!

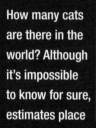

Feral cats are often afraid of humans

Feral Cats

Feral cats are also called barn cats, wild cats, or alley cats. A feral cat is a free-roaming cat that is lost, abandoned, or born and raised in the wild. Feral cats are usually afraid of people and will run and hide if they are approached. Most feral cats hide in daylight and come out to search for food in the evening. While life can be hard and short for feral cats, some become quite successful at making a living.

A stray cat, on the other hand, is a lost or abandoned pet that is not especially afraid of humans. He may hang out in places where people live or gather. Sadly, some pets are abandoned when their owners move, lose interest, or decide a cat is just too much bother or expense.

Feral cats cuddle together in a wheelbarrow on a cold night

Aundrea Hirschmiller
Rescue Champion

Twelve-year-old Aundrea Hirschmiller's main hobby is rescuing cats. After more than eight years of volunteering, she can no longer count the number of cats she has rescued. Aundrea works with a group called East County Animal Rescue in El Cajon, California. The group traps cats, spaying the females and neutering the males. It's not easy to capture a cat. Sometimes a mother cat will hide under a house with her kittens. When they decide it's safe, Aundrea crawls under the house to scare the mother cat out, while her dad waits with a net by the exit. Once the mother is captured, Aundrea gathers up the kittens. Aundrea also socializes the kittens, many of which have never been handled by a human. She says it's rewarding to transform a snarling kitten into a loving companion.

The CAT'S MEOW

What is TNR?
TNR stands for Trap, Neuter, and Release. Feral cats are caught and taken to a shelter or veterinary office. They're sterilized so they can't reproduce, given a health check, vaccinated for rabies (in countries where it is still a problem), and then released where they were caught. A released cat often has a notch removed from her ear to show that she has been sterilized.

Aundrea Hirschmiller

Feral cats appreciate a kibble meal

Cat Colonies

Feral cats sometimes get together where there is shelter and a nearby food source, like a large rodent population at a garbage dump. A cat colony is usually made up of groups of female cats, along with a few males, who stay in one area. You might find colonies in back alleys, parks, factory areas, and garbage dumps. The health of colony cats can vary; some may be healthy, while others could be flea infested and diseased.

ROME'S CATS

Cats have lived on the streets of Rome for thousands of years. Today you will find dozens of cat colonies, cared for by residents. One 20-year-old shelter, the Torre Argentina Cat Sanctuary, is located above a temple built more than 2,000 years ago. The cats attract tourists, who feed the cats or donate money for their care.

Large litters can keep cat populations high

Cat in the Torre Argentina Cat Sanctuary

Jennifer Aggio
Colony Champion

When Jennifer Aggio was fourteen, she found a scruffy, wounded cat in the ravine behind her home in Toronto, Ontario. She named him Lucky and started feeding him. Eventually Lucky allowed her to lift and cuddle him. She then took him to the vet, his fighting wounds were treated, and he was neutered and vaccinated. Jennifer knew that more feral cats lived in the ravine, so she continued to put out food and water. On advice from Toronto Cat Rescue, she began to conduct a Trap, Neuter, and Release program. Two years later, Jennifer estimates there are fourteen colony cats, many of them neutered. In addition to helping the cats right in her own backyard, Jennifer also volunteers at Ninth Life Cat Rescue. Jennifer's dream is to become a veterinarian and help save more cats like Lucky.

WHY SPAY OR NEUTER YOUR CAT?

The best reason for spaying and neutering is to prevent more kittens from being born, but there can be other advantages as well. Spayed females may be less likely to roam as they won't want to get out to find a mate. Neutered male cats also are not as likely to roam in search of females, spray to mark their territory, or fight with other cats.

Some street cats are beautiful and healthy

Jennifer Aggio

Cat shelters can be cozy, comfortable, and safe

Outdoor Homes

Throughout the world there are thousands of feral cats that experience harsh winters. They must endure extremely low temperatures, deep snow, and storms. Finding food and a warm, dry, safe refuge may be difficult or impossible. An outdoor shelter can make a huge difference. Shelters come in all designs, shapes, and sizes. I have seen effective cat shelters made out of hay bales, wood, concrete, and other materials. But every shelter should be:

- Located in a spot where snow won't build up or water won't flood

- Raised off the ground to keep the floor dry

- Insulated to help keep the cold out and the warmth inside

- Not too big; a cat's body heat must be enough to warm up the inside

- Have a doorway big enough for a cat but small enough to keep out other animals

- Include a door flap to keep out the rain, snow, and cold

- Be lined with bedding materials that won't absorb moisture

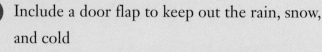

The Students of Clay High School and Dryden High School

Shelter Champions

The winters can be cold in South Bend, Indiana and in Dryden, Ontario. And the snow can be deep, which makes it difficult for a feral cat to find a warm, dry place to rest. So when local animal advocacy groups (the Second Chance Pet Network in Dryden and the Michiana Animal Alliance Group in South Bend) asked the high-school workshop classes to construct cat shelters, the students met the challenge. They built solid shelters with slanted roofs, which allowed rain and melting snow to drain off, keeping the interiors dry. The students say the projects have taught them a lot about construction, but more importantly, the shelters they've built will give some local feral cats a better life.

The Cat's Out of the Bag

If cat owners allow their cats to breed, they will be responsible for more cats than you think. In theory, 2 female cats who give birth to a litter of 8 kittens per year could produce as many as 175,000 descendants in just 7 years.

Dump cats eating some leftovers

Smart feral cats rest on shelter roofs

Shelter built by Clay High School students

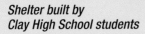

19

The cats of Cat Heaven Island

1,000 Cats Neutered

On March 25, 2012, Toronto Street Cats (TSC) hit a major milestone; they sterilized their 1,000th cat. That day, 53 cats were part of a TSC free spay/neuter clinic. The group, run entirely by volunteers, also organizes education events and activities to raise awareness of the plight of feral cats. They also host shelter-building workshops to teach people how to construct inexpensive outdoor shelters for homeless cats.

Japan's Cat Islands

Stray or feral cats are considered a problem all over the world. But there are places where stray cats are welcome. The small Japanese island of Tashirojima, also called Cat Island, is one of those places. The island's cat population greatly outnumbers its human population of 100. Cats are believed to bring good fortune and wealth, so they are fed and treated well. In the past, when island farmers raised silkworms, cats helped reduce the number of mice who ate the silkworms. The cats would come to the island's two villages and beg for food. Local fishermen would feed them scraps and eventually they came to see the cats as good predictors of weather. When one cat was accidently killed, the fishermen erected a small cat shrine called Neko-Jinja between the two villages. There are numerous other cat monuments on the island and even some cat-shaped buildings. Japan's second cat island is Fukuoka Island, also known as Cat Heaven Island, where the local fishermen and other residents feed and watch over the semi-wild cats.

The Cat's Out of the Bag

Most animal welfare groups support TNR programs to help control the cat population, but wildlife groups and some public health organizations believe cats who can't be adopted should be destroyed. They say cats kill too many birds and other animals, and pose a disease risk, especially in countries where rabies is still a problem. They also don't believe the effectiveness of TNR programs has been proven. Cat advocates disagree.

Jumping from boat to shore is a regular practice

It's feeding time at the beach

Eager for fish scraps, a cat leaps onto a boat

21

Shelters, People Who Care

Cat shelters should provide housing, food, safety, and veterinary care to abused, abandoned, lost, or unwanted cats. The shorter time a cat stays the better. A short stay means less stress, and a better chance of avoiding disease or parasites from other cats.

Every shelter is different. They can be bright, friendly places for both animals and people, or they can be dark and dreary. The cats may be housed individually in stacked kennel cages or they may be in rooms with sleeping boxes, perches, and other furniture.

Volunteers are essential to many shelters

Cute kittens are common in most shelters

Tiny kittens require special care

A clean, bright cat shelter facility

Most of the newer shelters seem to keep cats in groups of three or four, while some other shelters have much larger groups.

Cats who are brought to a shelter may be frightened and anxious, so being alone might be more comfortable. If, on the other hand, a cat stays for weeks or months in a shelter, being in a group might be far more interesting than sitting alone in a cage. At first, being with a bunch of strange cats may be stressful, but cats usually adjust to the situation. Most cats become comfortable in a group as long as there is enough good quality space, numerous perches, and concealed resting areas. A number of feeding and watering stations and litter boxes will also help cats get along.

23

Cats with space and good conditions

What Makes a Good Shelter?

I think every shelter should:

 Make the welfare and wellbeing of cats their highest priority

Make their shelter bright and cheerful

 Give every cat a thorough medical exam and vaccinations

Work hard to promote cat adoptions throughout the community

 Stay open during nights and weekends when people aren't at work

Spay or neuter every cat before they are adopted out

 Have a strict adoption process, including an adopter interview

Refuse people who want to keep cats permanently outdoors

Provide advice and assistance to anyone who adopts a cat

Reduce the number of cats who are put down

Work with cat rescue groups

Advocate to improve laws to protect cats

Harley Helman
Shelter Champion

When she was eight, Harley Helman decided that cats and dogs in local shelters needed some comfort while they waited to be adopted. Her project, called Blankets Fur Beasties, was born. Four years later, she still collects blankets, quilts, sheets, towels, pet toys, supplies, and food from individuals and businesses. Everything is taken to animal shelters and rescue organizations in the Cleveland, Ohio area. As of May 2013, Blankets Fur Beasties has donated more than 2,299 items. But Harley's contribution does not stop there. She is also calling for a law to make humane education part of the curriculum in Ohio schools. Harley believes there will be fewer animals in shelters and fewer cases of abuse and neglect if every student learns about the humane treatment and protection of animals.

The CAT'S MEOW

A no-kill shelter refuses to euthanize (put down) healthy, adoptable cats. If the shelter is full, workers look for foster homes or find other ways of dealing with additional cats. Sometimes shelters must wait to accept new cats until their current cats are adopted.

Harley Helman

Lou Wegner
Shelter Champion

When he was fourteen, Lou Wegner, an actor and member of the pop group Blonde, was in Los Angeles making a film. The director suggested Lou volunteer at an animal shelter. He was shocked to discover high-kill shelters, where animals are housed for only a short time before they are killed. That experience inspired him to found Kids Against Animal Cruelty (KAAC), one of the fastest-growing animal rights groups in the United States. Through Facebook and other

The Cat's Out of the Bag

High-kill pounds and shelters limit how long cats will be kept before they are put down, even if they are healthy. Sometimes if new cats are brought in and the space is needed, the cats already housed will be euthanized. Although no one knows for sure, it is estimated that in the United States alone, more than four million healthy, adoptable cats and dogs are destroyed each year.

KAAC crest

Campaigning for cats and dogs

Some quiet, fun time with cats

Media interviews spread the word about animal issues

social network sites, KAAC publicizes the plight of animals in high-kill shelters. So far Lou's group has helped rescue more than 20,000 animals. KAAC also promotes pet spaying and neutering and tries to educate kids about appropriate humane animal care. As of 2013, KAAC had chapters in 14 states, more than 18,000 Facebook Likes and 50,000 members, supporters, and associates worldwide.

27

Sarah Kuhnert

Socializing with cats is fun and helpful

Sarah Kuhnert
Volunteer Champion

Sarah Kuhnert was only nine in 2010 when she decided to help cats in her hometown of Grand Rapids, Michigan. She discovered Crash's Landing and Big Sid's Sanctuary, part of a no-kill cat rescue organization. At first she did extra chores at home, but that didn't raise enough, so when she sold Girl Scout cookies, she asked for donations. Just over a year later, Sarah donated $100 to Crash's Landing. That led to a second $100 donation and then cat food, treats, and other supplies. Since 2012, Sarah has volunteered at both facilities, cleaning, vacuuming, and doing other chores, followed by some cuddle time with the cats. She continues to ask for donations, but she also makes jewelry and crafts to sell at local businesses and craft sales.

Sarah and two new friends

Rachel Cohen
Shelter Champion

Rachel Cohen

When Rachel Cohen was nineteen, she had an amazing idea: Why not connect homeless teens with shelter animals? The teens would learn to care for animals, and the animals would get the love and attention they needed. In 2009, Rachel's inspired idea became Hand2Paw, a Philadelphia, Pennsylvania organization that helps service agencies and animal shelters develop programs for dozens of homeless teens and thousands of animals. Hand2Paw also conducts education programs aimed at teaching kids the importance of being kind to animals. Group sessions always end with everyone's favorite activity: Kitten Holding Time! The organization Rachel founded has expanded to provide volunteering and job placement with local businesses, giving homeless teens hope for a brighter future.

The CAT'S MEOW

Cat Sanctuaries

Cat sanctuaries are growing in number all over the world. Like wild animal sanctuaries, they provide a home for abused, abandoned, and unwanted cats in need. If good homes are available, then cats will be adopted out. But if homes are not available, the cats can live out their days at the sanctuary.

Some sanctuaries are small and operate out of a private home. Others are large and can house hundreds of cats with plenty of space indoors and out. A good sanctuary will make the physical,

A feral cat with Parliament Hill in the background

Volunteers looked after the Parliament Hill cats

psychological, and social needs of cats its highest priority. It will also make sure that cats are not overcrowded and that the standard of housing and care always remains high. They monitor the cats' health and provide medical attention, and work to minimize the risk of a new cat introducing a parasite or disease that could spread to others.

COOL CATS:
Scarlett

In March 1996, a fire broke out in an abandoned garage in New York City. When firefighters arrived to put out the blaze, one of them saw a little Calico cat pick up her kittens one by one and carry them to safety. Despite severe burns on her face, ears, paws, and fur, she kept returning to the burning building until she had rescued all her kittens. And then she collapsed. The firefighter took the mother and her kittens to a veterinarian. Scarlett, as she was now called, recovered and she became famous. Thousands of people offered to adopt Scarlett and her kittens, and all were soon placed in good homes. Scarlett lived with her adoptive family for ten more years, an amazing example of feline love and courage.

Scarlett looked different but she was a happy cat

Scarlett's face and ears were burned, but she recovered

31

Becoming A Foster Parent

A foster parent is someone who takes in a homeless cat on a temporary basis, until a permanent home can be found. Some foster parents also take in kittens who are too young to be adopted or cats who are ill, injured, or have special needs. Without foster homes, many shelters and rescue groups would find it difficult or impossible to operate.

It's a big responsibility to foster a cat, but it's rewarding work. Find out as much as you can about your foster cats, and what the shelter or rescue expects of you. But be warned—many people quickly fall in love with their foster cats and find it hard to let them go. Whether you keep your foster cats or let them go, you're a real Cat Champion.

Foster cats can be any age

Foster kittens play games and have fun

Sun Shibo
Foster Champion

Sun (Abu) Shibo is only seven, but that hasn't stopped him from helping cats. He lives in Dalian, a city in northeastern China, and he is one of the youngest volunteers for the animal protection group Pet 100. Abu and his mother visit an animal advocate to help her with the care and feeding of a number of feral cats. Abu also assists in finding forever homes for foster cats. He dances and sings at many Pet 100 parties to support the group's feral cat Trap, Neuter, and Release program and to raise money for animal protection.

Jordyn Arndt
Foster Champion

When Jordyn Arndt and her family discovered a litter of kittens behind their home in Farmington, Minnesota, they took the kittens to the rescue group Last Hope, Inc. But no foster homes were available, so the Arndts took on the job themselves. They kept the kittens in a separate room away from the other family pets, and Jordyn learned to properly care for and socialize the young

Sun Shibo

Jordyn Arndt

33

Cats feel safe in small, enclosed rest spots, like this box

Jasmine Polsinelli

kittens until they were ready to be displayed at the Last Hope Adoption Day at Petco. Soon Jordyn and her family fostered kittens regularly. When Jordyn was seventeen, she made use of her studies in graphic design to create promotional materials for Last Hope, including a new logo, business cards, signs advertising Adoption Days at Petco, and educational brochures. She even created signs for the cat crates!

Jasmine Polsinelli
Foster Champion

Ever since she can remember, eleven-year-old Jasmine Polsinelli has had foster cats and kittens in her home in Oshawa, Ontario. At one point she cared for twenty-one kittens! While having so many kittens sounds like a lot of fun, Jasmine learned it was a big responsibility; the kittens had been rescued from an animal hoarder's house and were sick, thin, and frightened. In addition to fostering cats, Jasmine and her mother have trapped many ill or injured feral cats, cared for them, and found them all good homes. Many of the cats and kittens were afraid of humans, so Jasmine worked hard to gain their trust. One of her foster cats spent three months hiding under a bed. But today the cat is healthy and friendly. Jasmine says, "Getting the chance to foster is the best thing to happen to me."

Kieran Zierer-Clyke
Foster Champion

Kieran Zierer-Clyke began fostering cats in 2008, when he was twelve. A local organization called Toronto Cat Rescue would bring feral kittens to his home in Toronto, Ontario. Life on the streets is tough, and some of the cats weren't used to being touched or handled, so it was Kieran's job to socialize them. Once a cat became sociable and friendly, Kieran and his family would begin the adoption process. Because of Kieran's dedication, a lot of cats have been given a chance at a happy life. Kieran says, "It's a good feeling when you sleep at night knowing there are fewer cats struggling to survive out on the street."

The CAT'S MEOW

Whether you foster cats or decide to adopt, remember that two or more cats are often better than one. Two cats will keep each other company, so they won't get lonely. Kittens from the same litter make the best friends of all.

Kieran Zierer-Clyke

Daniel Rademaker

Daniel Rademaker
Foster Champion

In 2008, when he was ten, Daniel Rademaker attended a Kentucky Humane Society summer camp in Louisville. There he learned how to care for shelter puppies and kittens. But his favorite activity was playing with the cats in the cat colony room. At home, Daniel asked his mom for a cat. But together they decided to become foster caregivers instead. In the three years since camp, Daniel has fostered more than sixty kittens until they've become old enough to be adopted out at the Kentucky Humane Society. It's hard to let the kittens go, but Daniel believes it's the right thing to do. Every year, more kittens are born; he knows there will always be a need for foster caregivers.

Socializing Cats

Most people don't want to adopt a cat that bites or scratches. It's much easier to take home a friendly cat. But foster champions like Sun Shibo, Jordyn Arndt, Kieran Zierer-Clyke, Jasmine Polsinelli, and Daniel Rademaker will tell you that socializing a cat isn't that difficult a job. Here are some tips to get you started:

- Speak softly and gently so they become used to the sound of your voice.

- Never chase cats or try to drag them out of a hiding place; instead, sit nearby for short "visits" until they are ready to come out on their own.

- Try not to frighten a cat as that may slow the socialization process.

- Use a variety of toys to get their attention and keep them interested.

- Try hand feeding; cats will become used to your smell and learn that you won't hurt them.

- Cats who don't like to be held may gradually get used to petting.

- Try touching or handling them, but start off slowly.

- Use different brushes to introduce grooming.

- Get down on their level; lie on the floor nearby and let them come to you.

- If a feral cat won't come inside, consider making a shelter against the house or in a doorway or garage. Provide a blanket or bed to curl up in, and leave food and water nearby.

- Make sure a feral cat can't be trapped indoors.

- Be patient! Every cat is different and some just need more of your time.

Adopting a Cat

Do I want a kitten with loads of energy, or do I want an older, calmer cat?

Do I want a specific breed of cat, or do I want a cat who used to be feral?

Should I consider more than one cat?

Does everyone in the family want a cat?

Who will feed and groom the cat and keep the litter box clean?

Can my family afford to pay for visits to the vet?

Do Your Homework

Some people think cats are easy pets that don't require much time or effort. But most cats do need some attention, so expect to spend at least an hour a day, and more for kittens and special needs cats. That time may be spent playing, grooming, or letting them just quietly sit on your lap.

You should also learn how to make your home cat-friendly and what your cat needs to stay physically safe and secure and psychologically healthy.

There are all kinds of sources of information, including articles, books, and websites. You can also talk to shelter and rescue workers, as well as veterinarians. If you want a specific breed, then a breed association should be able to inform you about the personality and health of that breed, along with any specific medical problems it might have.

You should consider taking time with any cat you're thinking of adopting. Many cat rescues will arrange for you to get acquainted with a cat. Some shelters have common cat rooms or special greeting rooms. If you're thinking of taking in a cat from a friend, ask a lot of questions and visit their house to see how the cat behaves. Remember, a new cat also needs a little time to get to know you before you go home together.

The Cat's Out
of the Bag

If you're a lost cat, what's the best way to make sure you are returned home? Carry your ID!

- Tags attached to a collar can include name, address, and phone number. But tags are easily lost or can fall off, and the writing could fade, so expect to replace tags often.

- License tags are required in some towns or cities, where the information on the registered cat is kept.

- Microchips are tiny devices no bigger than a grain of rice, which are injected under the skin. The information can be read with a special scanner. A microchip must be properly registered so the information can be kept on file.

- Ear tattoos will also identify a cat.

You've Chosen Your Cat. What's Next?

Shelters and rescue organizations want to be sure that their cats find good homes. So once you have decided on your cat, you and your family will be asked to answer questions on an adoption form. In most cases, the next step is an interview, usually in person but sometimes by phone. A shelter or rescue representative may want to visit your house. If your home is rented, you might have to prove that your landlord allows pets. A few shelters and rescue groups might also ask for references to make sure that you'll be a responsible cat owner.

The next step will be to sign a contract and pay an adoption fee. The contract outlines your

Ear tattoo on a shelter kitten

All cats should have a name or
license tag, microchip, or tattoo

responsibilities, such as spaying or neutering your
cat and providing medical care. The contract may
ask you to promise that you will keep your cat
indoors. The adoption fee can run from $20 or
$30 to $300. The fee helps to cover the costs of
running the shelter or rescue organization, so it's
money well spent.

WHY ADOPT AN ADULT CAT?

Kacey Rhinehart says, "Adopting an adult cat is just as good as adopting a kitten. Kittens grow up to be cats. Why wait?" Here are some other reasons for adopting adult cats:

• You don't have to wait to see how they will look or behave.

• They're calmer than kittens, so they won't tear up the house.

• They'll adapt quickly to the rules of the house.

• They know how to use the litter box.

• They can often be paired with another adult cat without too much bother.

• They're good for seniors or people confined indoors.

• They'll just relax or sleep when you're out of the house.

• They are wonderful, loving companions.

• Shelters have a difficult time adopting out adult cats, so you could be saving a life.

Kacey Rhinehart
Adoption Champion

After attending their summer camp in 2011, Kacey Rhinehart became a member of the Marin Humane Society's Animal Care Club in Novato, California. That's when she met Enzo, an adult cat who had been waiting for months to be adopted. The sixth grade student decided to point out the benefits of adopting adult cats. She started the Enzo Foundation and soon after, Enzo was adopted. In 2012, Kacey made videos for the two cats Fabrizio and Sheena, which were posted by the society through social media sites. Both cats soon found forever homes. Kacey's creative videos inspired the society to launch their first adoption commercial contest, in which local kids created short commercials about the animals at the shelter. As a result, adoption rates have increased substantially from the previous year.

Kacey
Rhinehart

The
Cat's
Out
of the Bag

Ever heard of Black Cat Syndrome? Cat shelters and rescue groups know all about it. The term is used to describe the lower adoption rate of very dark or black cats. No one knows why exactly. It could be that black cats are harder to see in shelter cages and don't attract attention to themselves. Maybe it's because black cats have been associated with witchcraft for hundreds of years, and some people still believe that black cats are evil and unfriendly, and bring bad luck. But there is some evidence to suggest that cat color might relate to cat behavior and resistance to disease; some experts believe black cats are a bit friendlier and healthier than other cats. Most of the black cats I've met have been very good-natured, so it may be true. If you are going to adopt, please consider a black or dark cat.

The
Cat's
Out
of the Bag

What is a kitten mill? Also called cat mills, these places breed cats for profit. The cats and kittens often share space with too many other cats, live in their own waste, and go without medical attention. Kitten mill operators advertise themselves as breeders but won't be able to provide registration papers or health certificates. Most kitten mill cats are sold in pet shops or from ads in the newspaper. Please help stop these mills by adopting from a local shelter or rescue, or from a registered, responsible breeder.

No Need to Buy a Cat

On September 21, 2011, the City of Toronto council voted to end the sale of live cats and dogs in pet stores. They became the second city in Canada to restrict the sale of pet-store animals. In 2012, Los Angeles, California banned the sale of cats and dogs unless they came from a shelter or rescue. About 30 other towns and cities have also restricted the sale of live animals. The primary reason behind most of these laws is that politicians didn't want to support animal cruelty by allowing

Not allowing pet stores to sell cats can help increase adoptions from shelters

stores in their town or city to buy animals from puppy mills or cat mills. They also wanted to reduce the motivation for people to breed more animals when there are already so many homeless animals in shelters and pounds. Encouraging people to adopt a cat or dog from their local shelter or rescue group will help reduce the number of homeless animals killed each year.

Ears pointed down show that a cat is afraid

Ears and whiskers pointing forward show he's interested in something

Cats like to be in control

WHAT DOES IT MEAN WHEN I...?

Here are some cat postures and what they mean:

When I lie on my back and stretch...I'm really relaxed.

When I sit on your papers... I'm pleased because I'm in control.

When I arch my back and fluff up my fur...I feel threatened.

When my tail is sticking straight up...I'm happy and ready to play.

When I wave my tail from side to side...I'm ready to attack.

When my ears point forward...I'm interested.

When my ears point down... I'm afraid.

When my ears turn sideways...I'm warning you that I'm ready to attack.

When I "knead" you, pressing my paws against you...I'm happy, calming myself, or leaving my scent so other cats know you are mine!

45

Indoors or Outdoors?

One of the biggest disagreements among cat lovers is whether cats should be kept indoors or allowed to roam freely outdoors. In the United States, a little more than 50% of companion cats are kept indoors. In the United Kingdom, the number is much less, possibly as low as 10%. Many humane societies and wildlife organizations suggest that cats should be kept indoors, but many cat advocates believe that cats should be given some freedom outside. I'm not going to tell you that cats should be indoors or outdoors. I'll leave that for you to decide.

Outdoor cats face more dangers than indoor cats

Leash walking a cat can be a great form of exercise

The CAT'S MEOW

Walkies, anyone? You can make the life of an indoor cat more interesting by taking him out for regular walks on a lead and harness. You wouldn't think that cats could be trained to walk on a leash, but many cats adapt quickly and enjoy the experience. A proper harness and lead are better for a cat than a collar, which could hurt his neck. And a cat can't escape from a harness.

Outdoors? Or Indoors?

If you are an outdoor cat, you won't be bored. You get lots of natural exercise; you can run, climb, dig, stalk prey, and roam around. You can meet other cats and explore and investigate whatever you want. And you can go home anytime for meals and attention. But…you might be injured by a hostile dog, cat, or wild animal. You might eat something poisonous. You could pick up a parasite or a disease. You might wander too far and become lost. And a car could hit you.

If you are an indoor cat, you may live longer than an outdoor cat. You will be warm and safe. You won't have to face other animals, and you'll never become lost. You'll be safe from cars. But… you could become bored and lonely. You might not get enough exercise and put on too much weight. And you might develop some bad habits.

What Does Your Cat Need?

If you decide to keep your cats indoors, this is what they will need:

- 🐾 A litter box (more than one if you have space or multiple cats) left in a quiet area
- 🐾 fresh water
- 🐾 scratching posts or areas where they can sharpen their claws
- 🐾 a place to nap
- 🐾 an elevated perching area
- 🐾 toys and playtime

Cats will seek out fresh water

Leave My Claws Alone!

Declawing is nothing like getting your nails clipped; it's a surgery in which part of the first joint of each toe is removed. Declawing is not a simple surgery, and cats who undergo it can spend many weeks recovering—some may have long-term complications or even lifelong pain. Declawing can also be done with lasers; a small, intense beam of light is used to burn through the toe joint. The procedure was developed because of the complications associated with surgical declawing. But some veterinarians say that a laser can be worse than the surgery, and cats can experience many of the same long-term effects.

Why do people have their cats declawed? Some people don't want their bodies scratched or the furniture ruined. Others believe that declawing will turn their cats into better pets. I think that if people value their furniture more than their cats, or if they can't spend time teaching their cats to use a scratching post, then maybe they should reconsider adopting a cat.

Declawing is most common in North America, but a number of American towns and cities, including San Francisco, Los Angeles, and Santa Monica, have banned declawing. In Canada, many veterinarians and most animal welfare groups oppose the practice, which they say causes pain and prevents cats from expressing normal behaviors. Twenty-five countries, including England, France, Germany, Austria, Switzerland, Japan, Australia, and New Zealand have banned declawing.

The Cat's Out
of the Bag

Why do cats scratch? In the wild, small cats often scratch the same locations over and over, each time leaving scent from the glands on their paws to mark their territory and warn other cats to stay away. Cats also scratch to sharpen their claws or simply to exercise.

Julia Eisen

S.T.A.R.T
ave the Animals Resc

Rachel Eisen

You've already met some amazing Cat Champions who care for cats by giving their time and energy. Now meet some champions who have made their contribution to cat welfare by raising money and educating others.

Rachel and Julia Eisen
Fundraising Champions

What's the best way to stop animal neglect and abuse? Rachel and Julia Eisen will tell you: make sure it never happens in the first place. Fourteen-year-old Rachel had already been volunteering at a vet's office for years when her twelve-year-old sister Julia joined her to help socialize stray or abandoned cats and kittens. It wasn't long before anyone in the area who'd found a stray animal or lost a pet would call the girls. In 2007, the sisters founded the BC Animal Welfare Society in Bergen County, New Jersey. Their main goal is to find good homes for the cats and dogs under their care, but the society also includes TNR, foster, and adoption programs, as well as education and financial aid to low-income pet owners. Together the sisters have raised more than $10,000 for their cause.

Zoe Albert
Fundraising Champion

Zoe Albert

Allen, Texas resident Zoe Albert believes only animals should wear fur. When she was eleven, she bought some fake fur and sewed it over the straps of her flip-flops. The result was such a success, her friends asked her to make some for them. By the time she was thirteen, Zoe had her own business called Faux Paws (*faux* is a French word meaning *false* or *fake*). Zoe's flip-flops, which she still makes by hand, are sold on her website, through a number of organizations, at pet adoption events, and in several stores. She's made more than $20,000, but she doesn't keep the profits—every cent goes to animal charities like the East Lake Pet Orphanage and Help for Helpless Animals.

Zoe sells her Faux Paws footwear

Evan Sweitzer

Evan Sweitzer
Fundraising Champion

It started out small in 2009. Evan Sweitzer saved up his allowance so he could make a donation to the rescue in Philadelphia, Pennsylvania, where he'd adopted his kitten Macha. The ten-year-old sent a short note and a donation of $46.75 to City Kitties. They posted his note on Facebook, and when people saw it, they sent donations too. Soon hundreds of dollars were raised. In 2010, Evan increased his donation to $86 by selling figs from his family's tree. In 2011, he donated $97, and in 2012 he raised $110. In January 2013, Evan appeared on *Ellen*, a TV show watched by millions across North America and worldwide. Ellen DeGeneres told him that the cat food company Fancy Feast wanted to help too. Then she presented him with a giant-sized check made out to City Kitties in the amount of $20,000!

Kiki Zhuang

Nai-Hui Zhuang

Education Champion

Seven-year-old Nai-Hui (Kiki) Zhuang waited while her mother attended a meeting about the NO FUR campaign of the animal protection group ACTAsia for Animals in Zhuhai, China. Kiki decided to help, so she took some NO FUR badges to pass out to her classmates. Kiki made a presentation to her class. She told them to inform their parents about the cruelty of the cat and dog fur trade in China and to ask them not to buy any fur products. Soon Kiki was speaking to the entire school. The principal invited ACTAsia to give a number of talks about animal welfare, and offered the school facilities for free education workshops. Kiki's single classroom talk has led to many school presentations throughout Shenzhen and Zhuhai as part of ACTAsia's Caring for Life Program.

The Cat's Out of the Bag

Around the world, the clothing industry still demands animal fur. And where wild animal fur is in short supply, cat and dog fur is sometimes used instead. The majority of cat and dog fur comes from China, which is the largest fur exporter in the world. Some of these products were discovered for sale in the United States. But the government has now banned the import of cat and dog fur. I hope other countries act soon to ban the import of products made with cat and dog fur.

Kiki is recognized for her work to help animals

53

The CAT'S MEOW

China did not pass a Protection of Wildlife Law until 1988. And they certainly need better laws to protect cats and dogs. But more and more people in China are standing up for the rights of companion animals. Organizations like the Chinese Animal Protection Network and Animals Asia Foundation are working hard to make life better for cats and dogs.

Cool Cat: Tuxedo Stan

Tuxedo Stan was once a stray cat who lived on the streets of Halifax, Nova Scotia. But his new owner, retired veterinarian Hugh Chisholm, saw how special his cat was, and he decided to use Stan to promote a spay, neuter, and cat care center in the city. To raise awareness, Stan became the face of the Tuxedo Party, and in 2012, he was proposed as a candidate for Mayor of Halifax. The campaign attracted a lot of attention and Stan became famous. He was featured in newspaper articles and radio and television shows around the world.

Tuxedo Stan never did get on the official election ballot because animals aren't allowed to hold office, but he did succeed in raising awareness about cat issues.

Support
Tuxedo Stan
Because neglect isn't working

www.tuxedostan.com

Tuxedo Stan

It's Up to All of Us

No matter who you are or where you live, you can make a difference in the lives of cats. I hope the Cat Champions in this book will inspire you to come up with your own ideas to help. Whether you decide to raise money, volunteer at a local rescue, foster or adopt a cat from a shelter, feed a colony of strays, or join an organization dedicated to helping cats, you could start saving lives today. Every effort will make a difference. Don't wait!

CRAZY FOR CATNIP

There's no doubt about it: some cats get positively silly when you give them catnip. They lick it, eat it, and roll around on it. The plant has a chemical in it called Nepetalactone, which affects between 50 and 70% of cats. Even some of the big cats, like tigers and lions, enjoy catnip. This sensitivity appears to be inherited, although you won't know if your cat is affected until they are older. Some veterinarians say you shouldn't introduce catnip to a kitten younger than 3 months.

The
Cat Lover's Pledge

- ❤ I will treat all cats with respect, compassion, and kindness.

- ❤ I will fully satisfy the physical, psychological, and social needs of the companion cats in my life.

- ❤ I will spay or neuter my companion cat.

- ❤ I will not mutilate my cat through the cruel practice of declawing.

- ❤ I will never tease, neglect, abuse, or hit a cat.

- ❤ I will adopt a cat from a shelter, pound, or rescue.

- ❤ I will contact a breed specific cat rescue group if I want to adopt a purebred cat.

- ❤ I will speak up for cats in my school and community.

- ❤ I will support the establishment of laws that protect cats.

- ❤ I will support organizations that work to protect both domesticated companion cats and cats in the wild.

Resources & Links

Here are some cat protection and information links, including links to all of the organizations mentioned in this book.

ACTAsia for Animals
www.actasia.org

Alley Cat Allies
www.alleycat.org

Animals Asia
www.animalsasia.org

BC Animal Welfare Society
bcanimalwelfare.com

Blankets Fur Beasties
www.blanketsfurbeasties.com

Canadian Federation of Humane Societies
www.cfhs.ca

Cat Advocacy, Rescue and Education (C.A.R.E.)
www.carecatswinnipeg.ca

Cats Protection
www.cats.org.uk/cats-for-kids

Chinese Animal Protection Network
www.capn-online.info/en.php

City Kitties
www.citykitties.org

Crash's Landing & Big Sid's Sanctuary
www.crashslanding.org

East County Animal Rescue
www.eastcountyanimalrescue.org

East Lake Pet Orphanage
www.elpo.org

The Ernest Hemingway Cats
www.hemingwayhome.com/cats

Faux Paws
www.fauxpaws.biz

Hand2Paw
www.hand2paw.org

Help for Helpless Animals
www.helpforhelplessanimals.net

International Fund for Cat Welfare
www.ifcw.net

Kentucky Humane Society
www.kyhumane.org

Kids Against Animal Cruelty
www.kidsagainstanimalcruelty.org

Last Hope, Inc.
www.last-hope.org

Marin Humane Society
www.marinhumanesociety.org

Michiana Animal Alliance Group
www.michianaanimalalliancegroup.org

Muskoka Animal Rescue
www.muskokaanimalrescue.com

Ninth Life Cat Rescue
ninthlifecatrescue.org

NYC Feral Cat Initiative
www.nycferalcat.org

Second Chance Pet Network
www.secondchancepetnetwork.ca

Toronto Cat Rescue
torontocatrescue.ca

Toronto Street Cats
torontostreetcats.com

Acknowledgements

I want to thank all of the amazing Cat Champions around the world who work to protect cats and improve their lives. Your efforts are greatly appreciated and truly inspiring. My thanks also go out to all the people who helped make this book a reality. It has been a collaborative effort and I hope that everyone who played a part in making it happen is pleased with the result. But most of all, I want to thank the cats and all animals for making the world such an enriching and remarkable place. I hope this book plays a part in making their lives easier, more enjoyable, and free from suffering.

Photo Credits

Title Page: boy with Cat Island cat–photograph courtesy of Fubirai / d.hatena.ne.jp/fubirai/ | Page 1: Hemingway cat–image by roboneal.com; three cats–photograph courtesy of Fubirai / d.hatena.ne.jp/fubirai/; ginger tabby (background)–photograph courtesy of Just for Kix Photography / justforkix.ca | Page 2: boy petting cat–photograph by Jo-Anne McArthur / weanimals.org; girl with kitten–photograph courtesy of Jennifer Meyer; kitten–photograph courtesy of John Spray | Page 4: ragdoll kittens–photograph courtesy of D. Butler; Ginger tabby–photograph courtesy of G. Featherstone | Page 5: Kieran Zierer-Clyke–photograph courtesy of Micah Zierer-Clyke; white cat–photograph courtesy of James Beaton | Page 6: cat falling–photograph courtesy of Fubirai / d.hatena.ne.jp/fubirai/; cat running–Shutterstock/©Sari ONeal; grass (background)–Shutterstock/©liseykina | Page 7: white cat jumping, black-and-white cat jumping–photographs courtesy of Fubirai / d.hatena.ne.jp/fubirai/; cat running–Shutterstock/©Sari ONeal | Page 8: arched back–Shutterstock/©Royster; lying on back–photograph courtesy of G. Featherstone | Page 9: cat in grass–Shutterstock/©LeniKovaleva; wide pupils–photograph courtesy of Just for Kix Photography / justforkix.ca; narrow pupils–Shutterstock/©Alexander Demyanenko | Page 10: Bengal cat–photograph courtesy of Just for Kix Photography / justforkix.ca; Canadian Sphynx–Dreamstime/©Svetlana Gladkova; Maine Coon, Persian–Shutterstock/©Linn Currie | Page 11: ragdoll kittens–photograph courtesy of D. Butler | Page 12: cat paw, cat on paper–photographs courtesy of G. Featherstone | Page 13: Hemingway cat–image by roboneal.com; Simon the War Cat–image courtesy of Michael W. Pocock / www.maritimequest.com | Page 14: looking through fence–Shutterstock/©nevenm; sleeping in wheelbarrow–photograph courtesy of John Spray; alley cats (background)–Shutterstock/©mysticlight | Page 16: cats and kibble–photo courtesy of James Beaton; yawning cat, Rome Sanctuary–photo courtesy of Andrea Schaffer / www.flickr.com/photos/aschaf/; kittens and mother–Shutterstock/©Afonia; three cats–Shutterstock/©Pavel Vakhrushev | Page 17: orange cat–photograph courtesy of John Spray | Page 18: raised cat shelter–photograph courtesy of Tara Anderson; kitten face–photograph courtesy of John Spray | Page 19: cats at dump, cats on shelters, shelters–photograph courtesy of Second Chance Pet Network / www.secondchancepetnetwork.ca; black-and-white cat–photograph courtesy of John Spray | Page 20: three cats–photograph courtesy of Fubirai / d.hatena.ne.jp/fubirai/ | Page 21: jumping to shore, feeding time, leaping onto boat–photographs courtesy of Fubirai / d.hatena.ne.jp/fubirai/ | Page 22: kitten with tilted head, two kittens–photographs courtesy of Kelli Polsinelli; volunteer with cat–photograph courtesy of Winnipeg Humane Society / www.winnipeghumanesociety.ca | Page 23: kitten care–photographs courtesy of Muskoka Animal Rescue / www.muskokaanimalrescue.com; cats in shelter–photograph courtesy of Jessica Thompson, founder of C.A.R.E. | Page 24: cats eating in shelter–photograph courtesy of Muskoka Animal Rescue / www.muskokaanimalrescue.com; cat through bars–photograph courtesy of Jessica Thompson, founder of C.A.R.E. | Page 26: cat behind cage–Shutterstock/©Bruno Passigatti | Page 29: Rachel Cohen with newborn, Rachel outside office–photographs courtesy of Ashley Smith, Wide Eyed Studios | Page 30: Parliament Hill cats–photographs courtesy of Stephen R. Gilman / www.flickr.com/photos/stephengilman/ | Page 31: the cat keeper–photograph courtesy of Vince Alongi / www.flickr.com/photos/vincealongi/; Scarlett full body, profile–photographed by Karen Wellen | Page 32: child holding kitten–photograph courtesy of Jennifer Meyer; mother and kitten–photograph courtesy of Muskoka Animal Rescue / www.muskokaanimalrescue.com; kitten looking out–photograph courtesy of Kelli Polsinelli; cat in sun (background)–Shutterstock/©Valerie Potapova | Page 34: cat in box–photograph courtesy of Jennifer Meyer; Jasmine Polsinelli–photograph courtesy of Kelli Polsinelli | Page 35: Kieran Zierer-Clyken–photograph courtesy of Micah Zierer-clyke | Page 37: boy petting cat, with mouse–photographs by Jo-Anne McArthur / weanimals.org | Page 38: cat with paw up–Shutterstock/©IrinaK; playing with toy–photograph courtesy of Just for Kix Photography / justforkix.ca; girl with kitten–photograph courtesy of Jennifer Meyer; ginger cat with black cats (background)–Shutterstock/©Liukov | Page 39: cat in cage–Shutterstock/©Martin Haas; cat in kennel–Shutterstock/©Michal Durinik; kitten in basket–photograph courtesy of Muskoka Animal Rescue / www.muskokaanimalrescue.com | Page 40: kitten with ear tattoo–photograph courtesy of G. Featherstone | Page 41: kitten group–Shutterstock/©Orhan Cam; cat in cage–Shutterstock/©Elina Pasok; Siamese with collar and tag–photograph courtesy of Florine Morrison; kid with cat–Shutterstock/©Suzanne Tucker | Page 42: sleepy Persian–Shutterstock/©Maria Meester | Page 43: Kacey and Enzo–photographs courtesy of Marin Humane Society / www.marinhumanesociety.org; black kitten–photograph courtesy of Angie Chauvin; black cat face–photograph by Jo-Anne McArthur / weanimals.org | Page 44: cat in pet store cage–Shutterstock/©kao; looking over the rail–photograph courtesy of Jessica Thompson, founder of C.A.R.E. | Page 45: cat with ears back–Shutterstock/©Krissi Lundgren; cat with intent look–Shutterstock/©Martina Misar-Tummeltshammer; Siamese cat lying–photograph courtesy of Florine Morrison | Page 46: black cat outdoors—Shutterstock/©kolessl; cat looking at raccoon—photograph courtesy of G. Featherstone; cat with toy mouse—Shutterstock/©MaxyM; cat with real mouse—Shutterstock/©David Lade | Page 47: girl walking cat—photographs courtesy of Nina Muller | Page 48: cat on tower—photograph courtesy of Lynn and Glenn Perrett; drinking from glass—photograph courtesy of Florine Morrison | Page 49: paws on ball–Shutterstock/©nalinratphi; cat on scratching post–Shutterstock/©Imageman | Page 50: kitten in daisies (background)–Shutterstock/©Tom Pingel | Page 54: Tuxedo Stan–photographs courtesy of Hugh Chisolm | Page 55: Tuxedo Stan–photograph courtesy of Hugh Chisolm; boy with cat–photograph courtesy of Jennifer Meyer; cat with catnip–Shutterstock/©itakefotos4u | Page 56: girl with kitten–photograph courtesy of Jennifer Meyer; tabby on fence (background)–Shutterstock/©Kachalkina Veronika | Page 58: cat on brick wall–Shutterstock/©Rostislav Glinsky | Page 61: boy with cat–photograph by Jo-Anne McArthur / weanimals.org | Page 63: barn cats in wheelbarrow–photograph courtesy of John Spray | Page 64: boy with Cat Island cat–photograph courtesy of Fubirai / d.hatena.ne.jp/fubirai/; all other cat champion photographs courtesy of their families; all other photographs courtesy of the author

Glossary

adoption
the process where a person agrees to provide a forever home for an animal

advocate
someone who takes on a cause or pleads a case on someone's behalf

black cat syndrome
a term used to describe the lower adoption rate of very dark or black cats

breed standard
a set of guidelines that define the physical qualities and personality of a specific breed

breeder
someone who raises animals to a breed standard, registers them, and provides a guarantee of health

cat colony
a group of feral or stray cats that live together in a particular area

catnip
a plant in the mint family that contains a chemical called Nepetalactone

champion
someone who defends or supports the cause of another

chatter, or chirp
a sound somewhere between a bleat and a meow

declawing
a surgical procedure that removes the first joint of each foot in order to ensure an animal's claws will not grow back

domestic cats
cats that have been bred for generations to bring out particular traits that make them more suitable companions to humans

dewclaw
a claw that has evolved and no longer functions or bears weight, found on the feet of some mammals

elliptical pupil
unlike a human's round pupil, a long thin pupil that opens up sideways

euthanasia
also called "putting down," the act of putting an animal to a pain-free death

felis catus
the scientific name that refers to domestic cats

feline
a cat, or anything related to cats

feral cats
also known as barn cats, wild cats, or alley cats, a free-roaming cat that is lost, abandoned, or born and raised in the wild

fostering
providing a temporary home for an animal until it is ready to be adopted

forever home
a home where an animal will live for its whole life, without being returned to a shelter

humane
kind, compassionate, trying not to inflict pain

hybrid cat
the offspring of a wild cat and a domestic cat

inherited
refers to characteristics passed on by one's ancestors

kitten mill
also called a cat mill, kitty mill, or backyard breeder, a business that breeds cats for profit with no regard to their health or wellbeing

Nepetalactone
a chemical found in catnip, which attracts and produces an ecstatic reaction in up to 70% of cats

neutered
a sterilized male animal whose testicles have been removed so he cannot produce babies

opportunistic predator
an animal that will kill all sorts of animals for food

PETA
"People for the Ethical Treatment of Animals," an animal rights organization

polydactylism
meaning "many-fingered," a genetic mutation that results in more that the usual number of digits on an animal's feet

predator
an animal that kills or preys on another animal, usually for food

rescue
refers to an organization that is dedicated to finding homes for stray animals

sanctuary
an area or place that is reserved for the care and protection of animals that are homeless or in need; a haven

shelter
an establishment, often supported by charitable contributions, that provides a temporary home for animals in need

socialize
to prepare an animal for human companionship

spayed
a sterilized female animal whose womb has been removed so she cannot produce babies

sterilization
the surgical removal of an animal's reproductive organs

stressed
anxious or fearful, which can affect the health of an animal

TNR
stands for Trap, Neuter, and Release (or Return), a method used of catching feral cats, sterilizing them, and returning them to the area where they were caught

trill
a sound somewhere between a purr and a meow

Index

Can you count how many cats are in the wheelbarrow?

* *Answer: We count thirteen!*

First published in the United States in 2014

Text copyright © 2013 Rob Laidlaw

This edition copyright © 2013 Pajama Press Inc.

10 9 8 7 6 5 4 3 2 1

www.pajamapress.ca   info@pajamapress.ca

The publisher gratefully acknowledges the support of the Canada Council for the Arts and the Ontario Arts Council for its publishing program. We acknowledge the financial support of the Government of Canada through the Canada Book Fund (CBF) for our publishing activities.

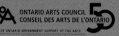

Library and Archives Canada Cataloguing in Publication

Laidlaw, Rob, author   Cat champions : caring for our feline friends / Rob Laidlaw.

Includes bibliographical references and index. For ages 8-12.
ISBN 978-1-927485-31-6 (bound).--ISBN 978-1-927485-54-5 (pbk.)

    1. Cats--Health--Juvenile literature. 2. Animal welfare-- Juvenile literature. 3. Animal shelters--Juvenile literature. 4. Voluntarism-- Juvenile literature. I. Title.

HV4743.L34 2013   j636.8'0832   C2013-902729-7

U.S. Publisher Cataloging-in-Publication Data (U.S.)

Laidlaw, Rob, 1959-
    Cat champions : caring for our feline friends / Rob Laidlaw.
[64] p. : col. photos. ;   cm.
Includes index.
Summary: A hopeful, inspiring look at the issues facing domesticated and feral cats, and the "Cat Champions" who are working to help them.
ISBN-13: 978-1-927485-31-6
1. Cats – Juvenile literature. 2. Feral cats – Juvenile literature.
3. Animal rescue – Juvenile literature.   I. Title.
636.8 dc23   SF447.L344 2013

Book and cover design–Rebecca Buchanan
Front cover photograph: boy with cat by Jo-Anne McArthur / weanimals.org
Back cover photograph: orange cat courtesy of John Spray

Manufactured by Sheck Wah Tong Printing Ltd.
Printed in Hong Kong, China.

Pajama Press Inc.
112 Berkeley St. Toronto, Ontario Canada, M5A 2W7
www.pajamapress.ca

Distributed in the U.S. by Orca Book Publishers
PO Box 468 Custer, WA, 98240-0468, USA

For all the cats and other amazing creatures we share this earth with.

R.L.